PETER KENT'S
CITY
Across Time

PETER KENT'S
CITY
Across Time

KINGFISHER

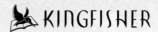
KINGFISHER

First published 2010 by Kingfisher
an imprint of Macmillan Children's Books
a division of Macmillan Publishers Limited
20 New Wharf Road, London N1 9RR
Basingstoke and Oxford
Associated companies throughout the world
www.panmacmillan.com

Illustrations by: Peter Kent

ISBN 978-0-7534-1897-0

Text and illustrations copyright © Peter Kent 2010
Copyright © Macmillan Publishers Limited 2010

9 8 7 6 5 4
4TR/0311/WKT/UNT/140MA/C

A CIP catalogue record for this book is available from the
British Library.

Printed in China

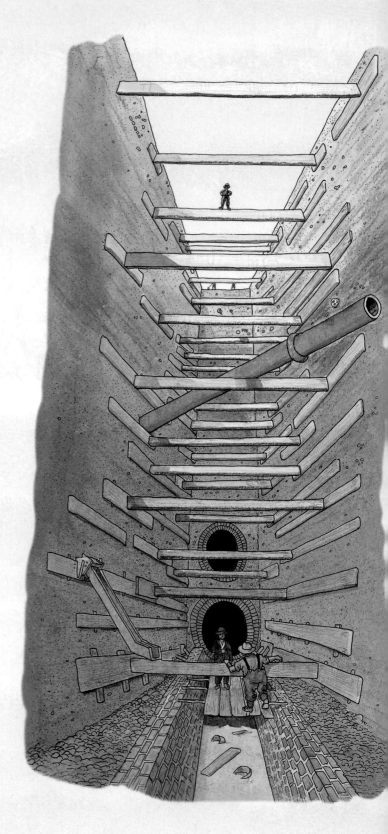

Contents

Introduction

Many towns and cities are very old. In Rome, Jerusalem, Damascus, London and other places, people have been living on the same site for thousands of years. Although most of the houses, shops and offices you see today are not much more than a century old, underneath them lie the remains of the buildings they replaced: layer upon layer of ruins mixed up with broken bits of household goods and rubbish. Each century leaves its layer of remains – like the age rings on a tree – the most ancient lying the furthest down.

The famous archaeologist Heinrich Schliemann demonstrated this when he dug into the hill that he thought was the site of the ancient city of Troy. He was proved right, but soon discovered that there were actually nine cities, each built on top of the remains of the one before.

This book cuts a slice through a city where people have been living for 10,000 years. Look carefully to see how the buildings people knock down and the rubbish they drop create the layers of history beneath their feet.

The first city was built around 3000BCE and the last was abandoned in 500CE. Can you imagine how many layers there would be if Troy was still being lived in today?

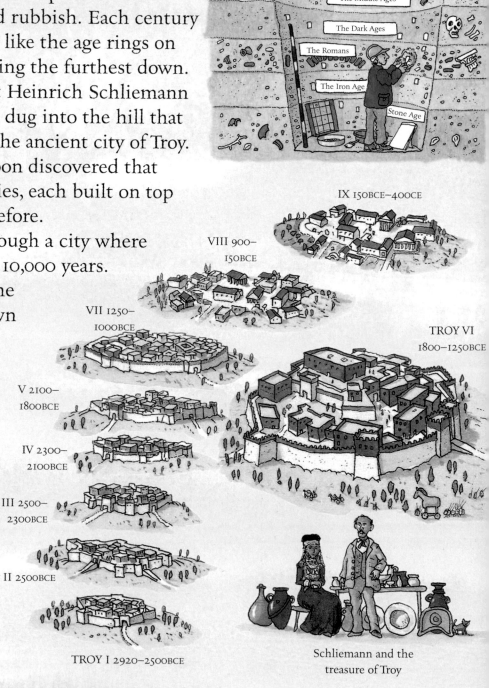

The 19th century
The 18th century
The 17th century
The 16th century
The Middle Ages
The Dark Ages
The Romans
The Iron Age
Stone Age

IX 150BCE–400CE

VIII 900–150BCE

VII 1250–1000BCE

TROY VI 1800–1250BCE

V 2100–1800BCE

IV 2300–2100BCE

III 2500–2300BCE

II 2500BCE

TROY I 2920–2500BCE

Schliemann and the treasure of Troy

Treasure trove

Archaeologists love rubbish, the more ancient the better. The objects they find in the layers beneath the city give valuable clues to dates and important events. A layer of ash tells us that once there was a great fire in the city; skeletons with the marks of sword cuts and arrowheads show war and massacre. But the real importance of the things archaeologists find is that they help us to understand how people in the past lived their ordinary lives.

When a Stone Age woman threw out a broken pot she did not realise that her rubbish would be carefully examined and glued back together thousands of years later. Even something very small, like a button, can tell us a lot about the people who made it. It gives us an idea of what sort of clothes they wore, how skilled they were at making things and, if it is not made of a material found locally, it tells us how far they travelled and traded.

Thousands of objects are buried beneath the city in this book, waiting to be discovered. If you look carefully through the following slices of the city you will find all the things on this page.

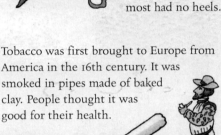

It was the fashion in the Middle Ages to have very long and pointed shoes. Some shoes were so long that they had to be tied to the leg with a chain. Shoes then were not made for left and right feet and most had no heels.

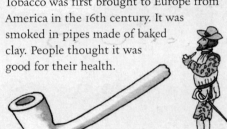

Tobacco was first brought to Europe from America in the 16th century. It was smoked in pipes made of baked clay. People thought it was good for their health.

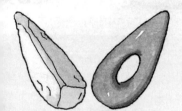

Stone axes from the Stone Age were not always rough and crude. Many were polished and ground to a jewel-like finish.

Pots have always been used for storing food in and eating and drinking from. Stone Age pots were made from clay and decorated with patterns. They were then baked hard in a kiln.

In the 17th century cannons fired solid iron balls. The largest weighed 29kg and were 200mm wide, but 8kg balls were more usual. They are still dug up from old battlefields.

In the Iron Age people displayed their wealth as jewellery. A rich person would wear magnificent gold necklaces and armlets called torcs.

The Romans were skilled at making stone and bronze statues. Some were huge, designed to stand on monuments or in temples, but many were small ornaments for the home.

Doctors and pharmacists in the 18th century made their own medicines. A blue bottle often meant that the contents were poisonous.

Digging down through history

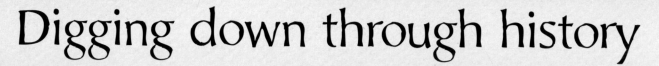

The people who dig to look for the remains of our history are called archaeologists. They love it when an old building is knocked down because then they get the chance to look at what lies beneath its foundations. They measure and make plans of any ruins and carefully excavate the soil to find as many objects as they can, all of which are carefully photographed and labelled. The archaeologists usually have to work fast because the owners of the site are impatient to start work on the new building, and when they do any ruins will be buried or destroyed.

A theodolite is used to survey the site and work out heights and levels.

A temporary office is used to store records and carry out scientific tests.

The sides of the excavation are drawn to scale and photographed.

A ground radar cart measures the depth of buried objects.

Pottery is washed and sorted.

It is very important to record exactly where everything is found and what it looks like, in order to work out how old it is.

A measuring pole is used to give scale in photographs.

Labels mark features such as floors and layers.

Small objects are carefully uncovered with trowels and brushes.

Sieve to collect very small objects.

9

The old Stone Age

The time before 2000BC is called the Stone Age because the tools people used then were made of stone. At the beginning of the Stone Age people travelled around the countryside with their possessions in search of food. About 10,000 years ago the last Ice Age ended and the great sheets of ice that had covered most of Europe and America retreated back to the north. The warmer climate encouraged small groups of people to move up from the south.

Many of the animals that roamed the land then – woolly mammoths, giant elks, woolly rhinoceros and aurochs (a large wild cow) – are now extinct. There were no cities. People moved over the land in search of food, living off wild plants and the animals they killed. They had no houses and lived in simple shelters made from branches or animal hides that could easily be taken down when it was time to move on. You can still find arrowheads and axes where they have left them and that is all that remains... except for their paintings.

Cave paintings

The people of Stone Age times did not usually live in caves – they were too dark and damp – but they did use them as secret temples and holy places. On the walls they painted beautiful pictures of animals and hunting scenes. These may have been part of a magic ceremony to make sure that there would always be plenty of beasts to hunt so that they would never go hungry. They used colours made from earth, mixed with animal fat, and they drew outlines with charcoal sticks or soot.

The new Stone Age

During the last part of the Stone Age people learnt how to grow crops and keep animals and so could live in one place. They built simple houses of wood, mud and thatch.

Stone Age people's knives, axes, spearheads and scrapers were made from stone – usually flint – and they had learned how to tame dogs to help them hunt. When they could not find enough flint on the ground they dug pits to mine it. Needles and small tools were made out of bone. Deer antlers were used as picks and oxen's shoulder blades as shovels. As stone and bone tools were lost or thrown away, they became buried underground. It is the remains of these objects that archaeologists look for today.

Cooking the Stone Age way

Just imagine how difficult it must be to cook without any metal pots or an oven. This is how it was done in about 2000BCE.

1. Wrap a joint of meat in straw.

2. Fill a huge trough with water and put the meat in.

3. Boil the water by dropping in red-hot stones.

4. After about 3½ hours the meat is ready.

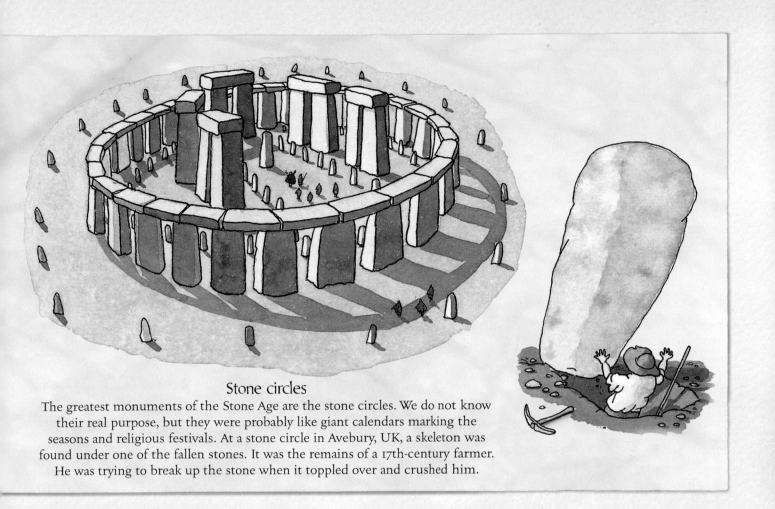

Stone circles

The greatest monuments of the Stone Age are the stone circles. We do not know their real purpose, but they were probably like giant calendars marking the seasons and religious festivals. At a stone circle in Avebury, UK, a skeleton was found under one of the fallen stones. It was the remains of a 17th-century farmer. He was trying to break up the stone when it toppled over and crushed him.

The Iron Age

In about 2000BCE people discovered how to make tools out of metal. At first they used copper but this was very soft. Then they learned how to mix tin with copper to make bronze, which was harder. In about 800BCE people began to make tools and weapons out of iron, which was the strongest metal of them all.

Iron Age towns were often protected by strong walls made of timber and earth. Houses were larger and more comfortable than they were during the Stone Age. People had learned by now to weave cloth and make beautiful jewellery in gold and silver. They sold their goods outside their town, and also bought goods from distant places. Money was used for the first time instead of swapping goods. Iron bars were used as money at first but later they were replaced by gold coins.

Blue tattoos
The people of the Iron Age painted or tattooed themselves with intricate swirling patterns drawn in a blue vegetable dye called woad.

War chariots
Chariots were used in Iron Age warfare. Warriors ran down the harness pole of the chariot as it was driven at full speed, ready to fight their enemies.

Ancient Roman times

B y about 100CE the mighty Romans had conquered most of Europe and made it part of their vast empire. The Romans put up the first buildings in brick and stone in what is now Britain and France.

A Roman town had a central market and meeting place called a forum, a town hall, many shops, paved streets and public baths with hot water and central heating. The bigger towns had several temples, and an amphitheatre where games and fights between gladiators took place. The Romans knew that clean people are healthier and they built proper sewers and organized a good supply of fresh water in towns.

Smelly pots
Although the Romans were keen on keeping clean, their blocks of flats (below left) must have been very smelly. There were no toilets and urine was collected in big pots at the bottom of the stairs. The urine was sold to clothmakers to stiffen fabric.

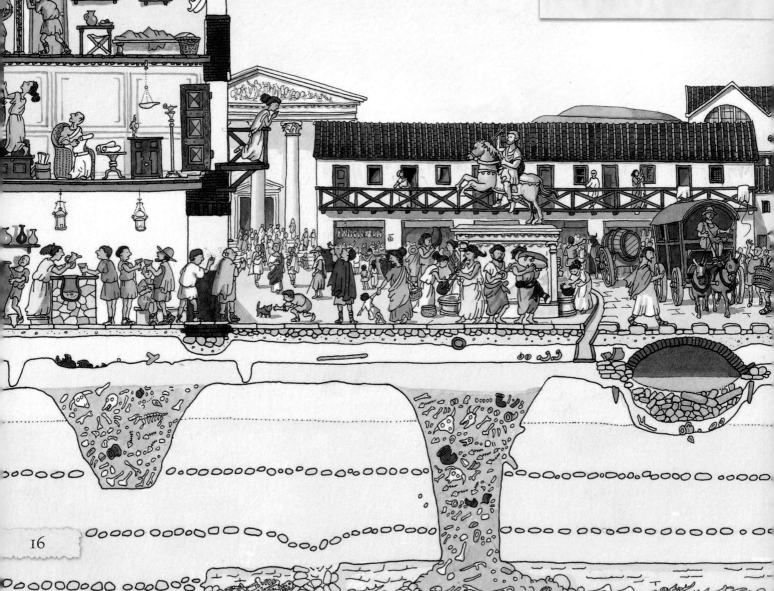

Keeping out burglars

The Romans did not have a proper police force and were worried about being burgled. They built their houses with only a few windows on the walls facing the street and fitted doors with complicated locks. In many houses the door was jammed shut with a pole.

Household gods

Every Roman home had a shrine and an altar dedicated to the household gods. The head of the family made an offering there every day to keep in favour with them.

Waiting for water

Only the richest houses had water piped directly into them. Most people got their water from public fountains. These must have been very social places where people gossiped as they queued.

17

The catacombs

The Romans did not allow the dead to be buried inside the city, so all cemeteries were outside the city walls. Bodies were cremated or burnt on a pyre and the ashes placed in a special jar called an urn.

A secretive sect, who worshipped the god Mithras, met in underground temples (left). The chief worshippers dressed up as lions and ravens to make offerings to Mithras, who was always shown killing a bull.

The Christians were not popular at first in Rome. Many were persecuted because they would not worship the pagan gods. They were forced to hold services in secret, hidden away deep in the catacombs (below).

The urns were placed inside or under beautiful monuments that were often decorated with a statue or bust of the dead person.

When space ran out, underground cemeteries called catacombs were built. Long passages were excavated and the funeral urns were placed in niches in the walls, rather like books on a shelf. Richer people had large chambers where the whole family could be buried.

The ashes in a funeral urn were placed in a prepared niche during a solemn ceremony.

19

The Dark Ages

In the fifth century CE the Roman empire, which had been growing weaker for a century, was invaded by tribes known as barbarians from northern Europe. The barbarian tribes that settled within the old empire – the Goths, Franks and Saxons – did not want to live in the Roman towns and the buildings quickly fell into ruin.

The barbarians could not build with stone at first and their houses were usually made of wood with thatched roofs. The most important building in any village was the hall of the chief or 'thegn,' where he lived with his warriors.

Stone crosses
The barbarians were pagans, worshipping many gods, until they were converted to Christianity. One of the first things the Christians did was to erect a stone cross, normally on the site of a pagan holy place. This is where the church was built later.

Saxon treasure

The Saxons were skilled jewellery makers. Wealthy men and women wore splendid brooches, clasps and pendants. These were often made of gold and decorated with glass or coloured stones.

Learning to build

When the Franks and the Saxons began to build in stone in about 700CE they copied the Roman ruins around them. Their early attempts were far less sophisticated than the Romans'.

The Middle Ages

During the Middle Ages (roughly 1000 to 1500CE), towns grew and became rich again. Over much of Europe the houses were made of wooden frames with plaster walls. Only castles, churches and the houses of the very wealthy were built of stone. The streets were often unpaved, with open drains, and it was difficult to keep the town clean. Animals wandered about and people threw rubbish out of their windo[w]

The market place was very important. People came in from the cou[ntry] to sell food and buy goods made in the town. Shops were simple room[s] that opened out onto the street. Almost all of the things people sold in them were made in the house behind.

Football

A favourite street entertainment was football. Sometimes hundreds played in one game! It was noisy and dangerous – houses were damaged and people killed.

Miracle plays

People were very religious during the Middle Ages and celebrated holy days with feasts and festivals. Miracle plays were popular and groups of townsfolk would club together to put on a particular scene.

A medieval mine

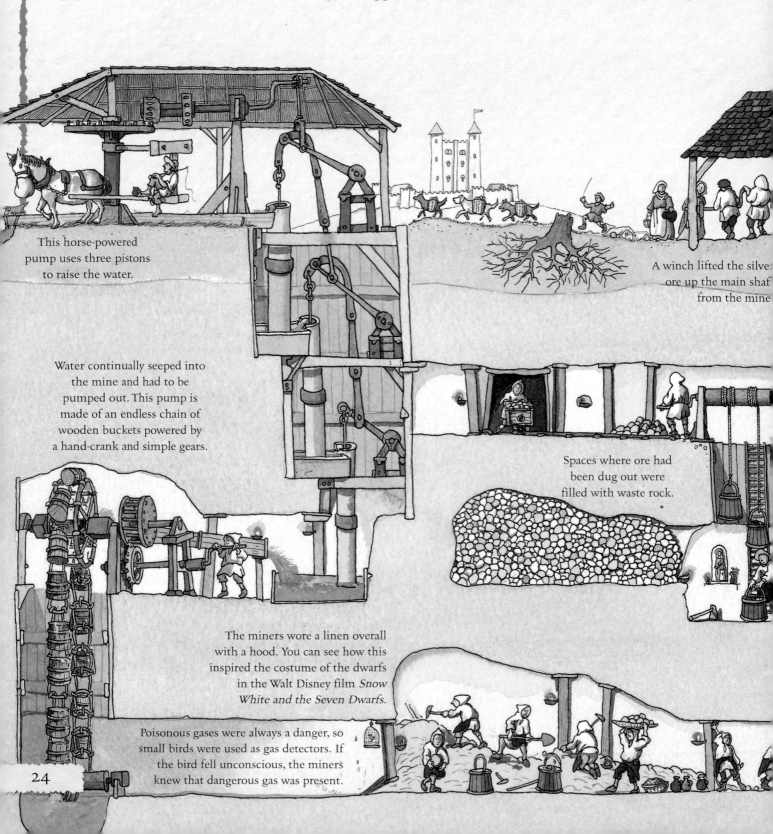

Mining has always been a dirty and dangerous job, ever since the new Stone Age when men dug deep into chalk for the biggest and best flints. Ancient Egyptians mined gold and the Romans dug for copper, gold, iron and lead all over their empire. In the Middle Ages the most skilful miners were to be found in Germany, where they invented many ingenious machines to make their work easier. This picture

This horse-powered pump uses three pistons to raise the water.

Water continually seeped into the mine and had to be pumped out. This pump is made of an endless chain of wooden buckets powered by a hand-crank and simple gears.

The miners wore a linen overall with a hood. You can see how this inspired the costume of the dwarfs in the Walt Disney film *Snow White and the Seven Dwarfs*.

Poisonous gases were always a danger, so small birds were used as gas detectors. If the bird fell unconscious, the miners knew that dangerous gas was present.

A winch lifted the silver ore up the main shaft from the mine.

Spaces where ore had been dug out were filled with waste rock.

shows a silver mine. Miners had to dig deep to reach the precious ore – the rocks that contained the silver. Coal mining did not become important until most of Europe's forests had been cut down and burnt as fuel.

A water-powered fan drew fresh air down the shaft to enable the miners to breathe.

The silver was present in the ore, which had to be brought to the surface and crushed.

The first railways were used in German mines. The rails and wheels of the trucks were made of wood.

A fire was lit to get air moving through the tunnels.

The miners climbed up and down the shaft on ladders. Sometimes they slid down poles, or even down a leather carpet.

Before drills and explosives were invented, miners split large rocks using wooden wedges.

Props made of wood held up the roof. Often they bent or broke under the weight of the rocks above.

The mine was lit by simple oil lamps.

The 16th century

By the 16th century houses were larger and had chimneys, instead of just a hole in the roof. Most windows were filled with glass for the first time instead of being closed with wooden shutters. Although still built mainly from wood, houses were more comfortable and contained more furniture and ornaments.

The city streets were still unpaved, dirty and littered with rubbish. At night the city was dark and often dangerous. Fresh water was taken to houses by a person who worked as a water-carrier or fetched by the family from a fountain (unless a house had a well). There were no proper drains and during the summer the city was very smelly and unhealthy.

26

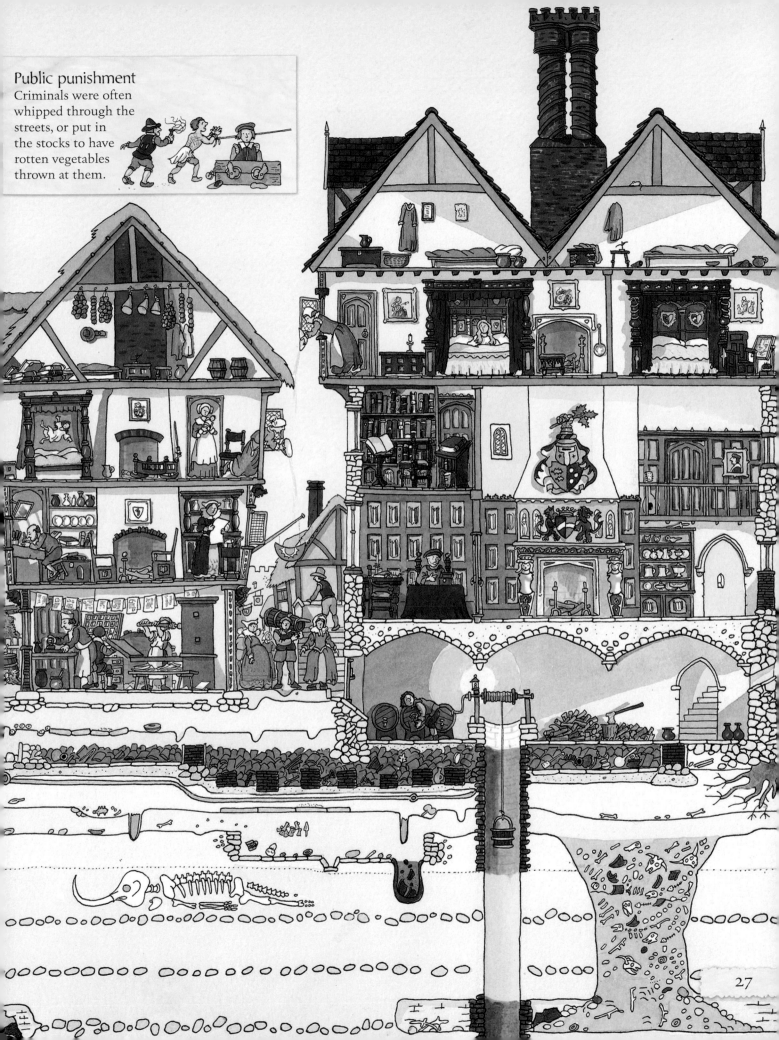

Criminals were often
whipped through the
streets, or put in
the stocks to have
rotten vegetables
thrown at them.

27

The 17th century

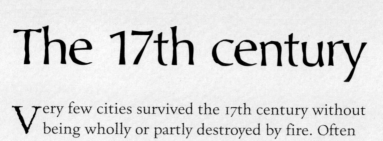

Very few cities survived the 17th century without being wholly or partly destroyed by fire. Often the cause was accidental, but many cities were burnt down after being bombarded or captured by enemies. Soldiers who captured cities also badly damaged them as they searched every house for things to steal.

Outbreaks of plague killed thousands of people. The plague was spread mainly by rats who made their nests in the wooden houses and fed on the rubbish that lay in the streets.

Fire fighting
Long hooks pulled burning thatch off roofs. Fire engines were just hand-pumps.

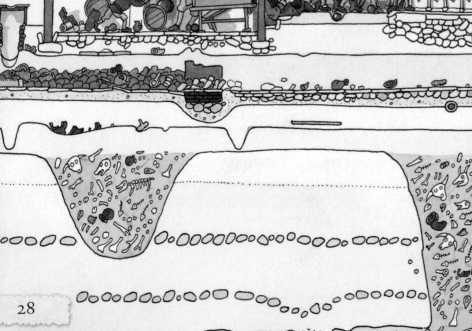

Plague pits
So many people died from the plague that they were buried together in huge pits.

The 18th century

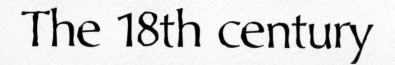

The great fires of the 17th century meant that many cities were almost completely rebuilt in the 18th century. Most of the old wooden buildings were replaced by houses built in brick and stone. This new style of architecture was based on copies of Roman buildings. Streets were properly paved and parts of the city began to be less cramped as wide streets and broad squares were built.

Sedan chairs
Wealthy people took a sedan chair through crowded city streets. They could be hired like taxis can today.

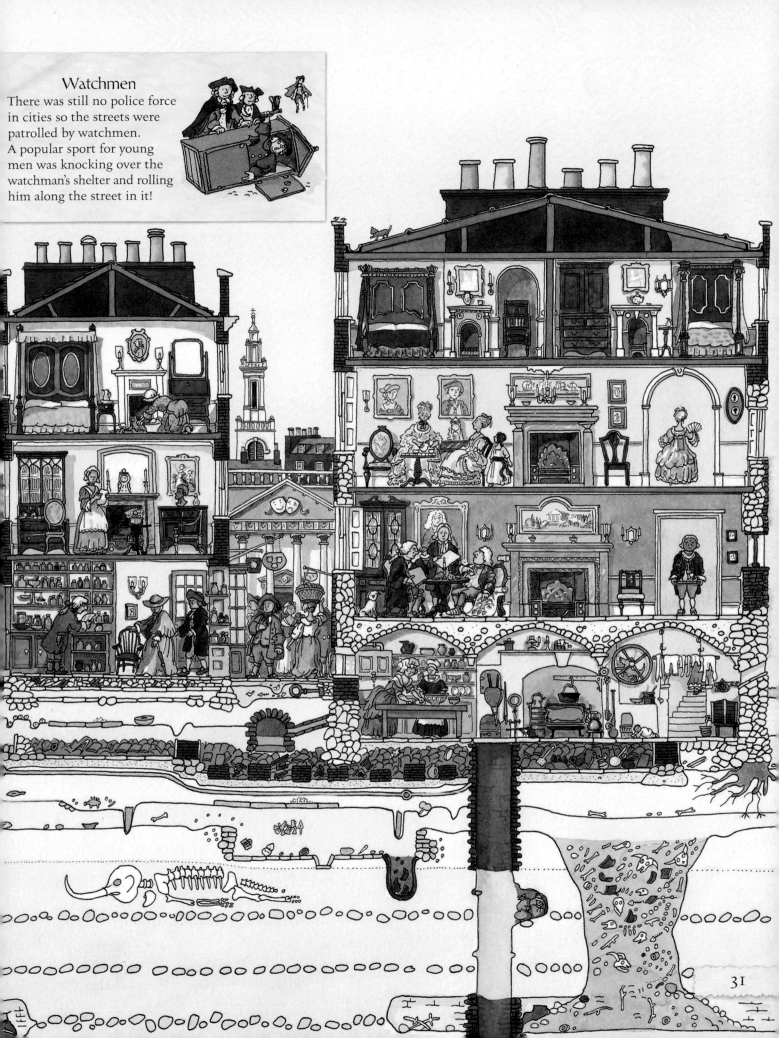

There was still no police force
in cities so the streets were
patrolled by watchmen.
A popular sport for young
men was knocking over the
watchman's shelter and rolling
him along the street in it!

31

The 19th century

During the 19th century cities changed more than at any other time in their history. They grew much larger and all sorts of different buildings were constructed. There were railway stations, concert halls, libraries, offices and schools. The streets were properly paved and brightly lit by gas lamps. Underground pipes carried gas and water into the city and sewage out of it. Cities became healthier and less smelly places to live in, but they suffered from a new problem – traffic jams!

An underground railway

One hundred and fifty years ago the streets of London were crammed with horse-drawn carts, carriages and buses. They moved at a crawl and the noise and smell was overpowering. Something needed to be done or the streets would be jammed solid. A network of undergound roads in tunnels lit by gaslight was suggested, but the police objected: thieves and muggers would lurk in the shadows.

BOVA

VITA

A better solution was an underground railway beneath the overcrowded streets to carry workers smoothly into the city. It took nearly 20 years to plan and build the Metropolitan, the world's first underground railway. It was 6km long and, when it opened in 1863, was an instant success.

The railway was only 10m underground and built by the 'cut and cover' method. A deep trench was dug, the rails laid and then a brick arch built to complete the tunnel. The trains were pulled by steam locomotives that were supposed to be smokeless but still filled the tunnels with choking fumes. At stations there were openings to the streets above to let in light and air.

Small railway carriages powered by compressed air carried mail bags in a tube beneath the streets at a speed of 10 km/h.

Lines deep underground were impossible to use with steam locomotives and had to wait until new methods of tunnelling and electric trains were invented (right). The first deep line or 'tube' opened in London in 1890. The carriages had no windows – as there was nothing to look at – and were pulled by little electric locomotives. Later lines had trains of carriages with electric motors – like the ones today.

35

The 20th century

During this century, wars and rebuilding destroyed many old buildings. Some of those that remained were altered to suit new uses. Below the streets more tunnels carried extra drains and electricity, telephone and television cables.

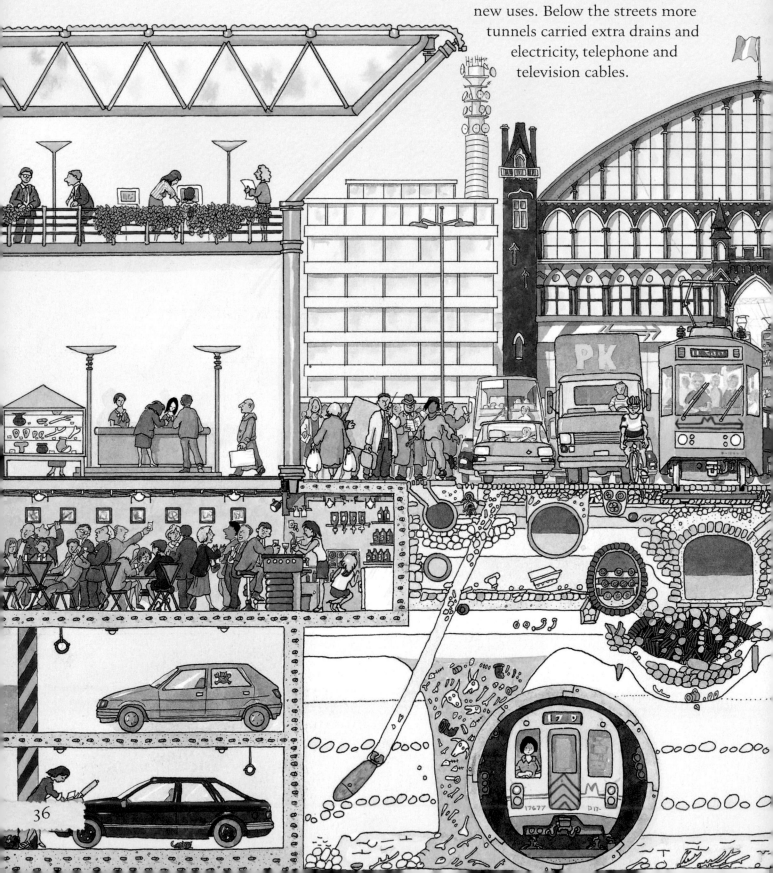

Some cities developed a public railway system deep underground in tunnels. Many buildings rose to great heights, with deep foundations to support their weight. Builders digging these foundations sometimes help archaeologists by finding ancient remains in the oldest parts of the cities.

37

Secret bunker

For over 40 years from 1945, the USA and other Western powers confronted the USSR in what was known as the Cold War.

Both sides threatened each other with atomic bombs powerful enough to destroy whole cities. Huge bunkers were built deep underground where people would be safe from the blast and deadly radiation. It was far too expensive to build shelters like this for everyone, but it was important to make sure that the government and military command would survive so that there would not be complete chaos after the bombs had dropped.

Entrance one

Underground railway

Dormitory

Canteen

Kitchen

Recreation room

This bunker in a secret location was made of two parallel tubes 40m below the ground. There was room for about 500 people and all the communication equipment they would need to keep in contact with other bunkers and keep the country running. They had supplies for up to six months as it would have been too dangerous to come to the surface any sooner.

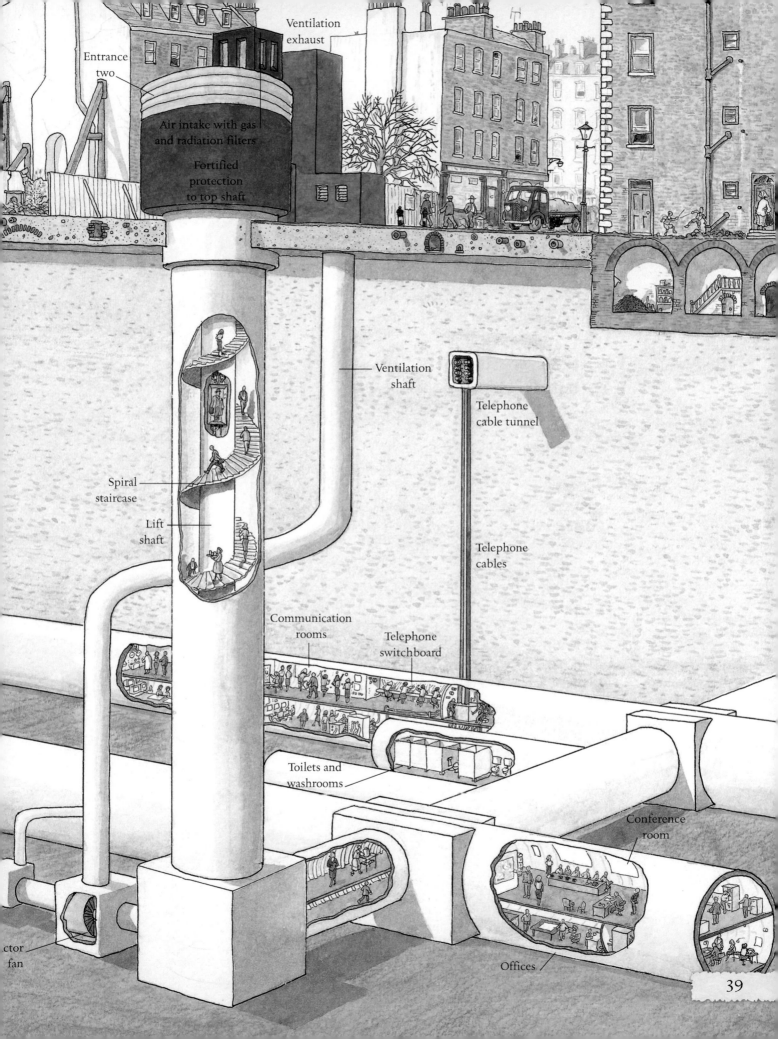

Entrance two

Ventilation exhaust

Air intake with gas and radiation filters

Fortified protection to top shaft

Ventilation shaft

Telephone cable tunnel

Spiral staircase

Lift shaft

Telephone cables

Communication rooms

Telephone switchboard

Toilets and washrooms

Conference room

...ctor fan

Offices

39

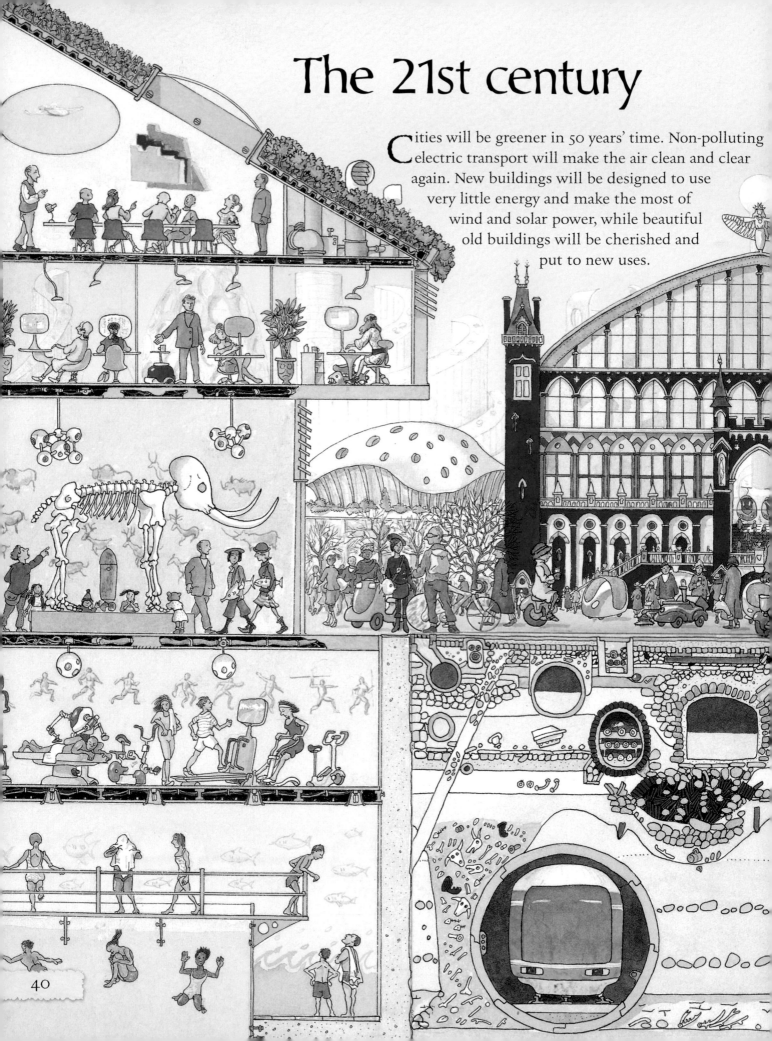

The 21st century

Cities will be greener in 50 years' time. Non-polluting electric transport will make the air clean and clear again. New buildings will be designed to use very little energy and make the most of wind and solar power, while beautiful old buildings will be cherished and put to new uses.

The city will remain much the same: a place to live, work, shop and be entertained – just as it was in the Stone Age.

41

The far future

Who knows what our city will look like in 10,000 years? Perhaps war or climate change will have destroyed it so completely that nothing remains on the surface except the stumps of mighty buildings, weathered and overgrown to look like hills.

But if, even further in the future, civilization starts again or aliens arrive to explore the planet, the archaeologists of the distant future will find plenty to keep them busy as they cut a slice through what used to be a city.

Glossary

Archaeology

Mithras

Archaeology The study of the past by digging up objects and remains of buildings.

Barbarians The tribes who lived outside the borders of the Roman empire and who appeared rough and uncivilized to the Romans.

Mithras A sun god from ancient Persia. He is usually shown as a young man wearing a pointed cap and killing a bull. His worshippers met in underground temples and dressed up as lions and ravens for their secret ceremonies. Nobody worships Mithras nowadays, which is probably a good thing.

Bunker An underground shelter made of reinforced concrete or some other material strong enough to resist bombs and shells.

Catacomb An underground cemetery. A catacomb has long tunnels with tombs and chambers for burials dug into the sides. Catacombs are very useful for burying large numbers of people without taking up too much room above ground.

Ore

Niche A shallow recess in a wall designed to hold a statue, vase or ornament.

Ore A rock that contains particles of some useful material like iron, copper or gold. Usually it has to be crushed or melted to separate the metal from the useless rock.

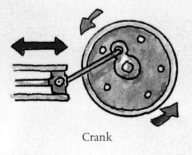
Crank

Crank Part of an axle bent at a right angle. It is useful for changing backwards and forwards or up and down movement into circular motion – like the pedals on a bike.

Foundations The lowest part of a building that gives firm support to the walls.

Pagan

Pagan Someone who doesn't believe in Christianity or one of the other major religions. The pagans in the past worshipped many gods and goddesses, like Jupiter, Mercury, Thor and Freya.

Locomotive

Locomotive An engine that moves about under its own power, usually applied to the engine that pulls a train along a railway line. Locomotives are powered by electricity, diesel, steam and, occasionally, compressed air.

Pendant An ornament usually attached to a necklace, chain or chord and hanging down over the chest.

Pharmacist A person who makes up and sells medicinal drugs. They are commonly, and wrongly, known as chemists.

Pharmacist

Plague A rapidly spreading infectious disease. Usually it refers to bubonic or pneumonic plague: the Black Death of the Middle Ages that killed about one-third of all the people in Europe and kept recurring until the 19th century.

Pyre A pile of wood on which to burn a dead body.

Pyre

Radar A device to detect objects by sending out radio waves. When these hit something solid they bounce back and the machine can read the signals to work out the size, shape and position of the object. Radar is mostly used by planes and ships but archaeologists find it very useful to detect things underground.

Sewage Technically anything carried in a sewer or underground channel but it usually means human waste.

Shaft A vertical or sloping entrance to a mine. The vertical shafts of gold mines in South Africa are up to 3,000m deep.

Shaft

Shrine A place for religious objects and holy statues where people pray and make offerings to the gods.

Solar power Electricity made from the heat and light of the sun.

Switchboard In an old-fashioned telephone system every phone had a wire that led to a board where it ended in a socket. If you wanted to speak to another phone, the girl – and it usually was a girl – plugged a wire into your socket and then plugged it into the socket of the number you asked for and the connection was made.

Switchboard

Theodolite An instrument with a rotating telescope used by surveyors to measure horizontal and vertical angles. It is essential when setting out the levels for new roads and buildings.

Treasure trove A find of buried valuables. In UK law it means a discovery of gold and silver articles that have been hidden by an unknown owner who expected to come back and dig them up again. Things that have just been lost are not treasure trove. All finds of treasure trove must be reported.

Treasure trove

Urn A vase, usually rounded with a foot, used for storing the ashes of a dead body.

Winch A machine for lifting in which the rope or wire is wound round a roller or drum. Another name for this is a windlass.

Shrine

Winch

Index

Further information

Digging down through history

There are digs going on all the time all over Britain. Most welcome visitors and often need volunteers to help. For a complete list and to see if there is one near you, contact your local museum or go to:
http://archaeology.about.com/od/ukdigs/Archaeology_Digs_in_the_United_Kingdom_and_Ireland.htm

The old Stone Age

There aren't many sites with much to see in Britain, but France has some of the most beautiful and impressive cave paintings. Most are in southwest France. The most famous cave at Lascaux is closed to the public, but a replica has been built and there are plenty more caves to visit – see:
www.lascaux.culture.fr/

The new Stone Age

If you want to go down a real Stone Age flint mine, visit Grime's Graves near Thetford in Norfolk:
www.english-heritage.org.uk/daysout/properties/grimes-graves-prehistoric-flint-mine/

The Iron Age

At Castell Henllys near Newport in Wales, an Iron Age fort has been rebuilt with ramparts, round houses and a granary. It's well worth a visit to experience what life was like in 500BCE:
www.pembrokeshirecoast.org.uk/default.asp?PID=397

Ancient Roman times

There are Roman remains all over Britain and Europe. After London was bombed in the Second World War, a lot of the Roman city was revealed beneath the ruins of modern buildings, including a complete temple of Mithras which you can visit at Queen Victoria Street. The Museum of London has great Roman displays and you can see part of the wall the Romans built to defend the city:
www.museumoflondon.org.uk/English/

The catacombs

The only catacombs you can see in Britain are ones in Victorian cemeteries such as Highgate, in London – very spooky. The best ones are, of course, in Rome, Italy, where you can also see more underground temples of Mithras:
www.catacombe.roma.it/en/storia.html

The Anglo-Saxons

If you want to experience Saxon life go to the rebuilt Anglo-Saxon village at West Stow near Bury St Edmunds. There are Saxon houses and workshops and even farm animals and people in costume:
www.stedmundsbury.gov.uk/sebc/play/weststow-asv.cfm

A medieval mine

One of the best preserved medieval mines in the world is the World Heritage site of Banska Stiavnica in Slovakia. Krakow in Poland has amazing salt mines with over 1,000km of tunnels up to 300m below ground. There is even a chapel with altar, candlesticks and statues all carved out of salt. For a good list of historic mines to visit, see:
www.erih.net/index.php?id=98&user...1&L=0...

Medieval to modern times

Most cities have a museum with good displays of archaeological finds and artefacts from all ages. At York (www.yorkcastlemuseum.org.uk) they have reconstructed a complete Victorian street, and at Beamish Museum, County Durham, there is a working slice of 19th century Britain complete with a mine, steam trains, shops and trams:
www.beamish.org.uk

An underground railway

The first underground railway is now part of the Circle Line on the London Underground. The station that has changed least is Baker Street, which is well worth a visit:
http://en.wikipedia.org/wiki/Baker_Street_tube_station

Secret bunker

For more information on these mysterious places, visit Subterranea Brittanica:
www.subbrit.org.uk
or www.bunkertours.co.uk/belsize_park.htm

The 21st century

To see a variety of buildings being planned for the future, go to:
www.ft.com/cms/s/0/089feb28-baa3-11df-b73d-00144feab49a.html#axzz1HRTD31j5